joy

Written & compiled by M.H. Clark ♦ Designed by Jessica Phoenix

COMPENDIUM™
INCORPORATED

ACKNOWLEDGEMENTS
These quotations were gathered lovingly but unscientifically over several years and/or were contributed by many friends or acquaintances. Some arrived—and survived in our files—on scraps of paper and may therefore be imperfectly worded or attributed. To the authors, contributors and original sources, our thanks, and where appropriate, our apologies. –The Editors

WITH SPECIAL THANKS TO
Jason Aldrich, Gerry Baird, Jay Baird, Neil Beaton, Josie Bissett, Laura Boro, Melissa Carlson, Tiffany Parente Connors, Jim & Alyssa Darragh & Family, Rob Estes, Pamela Farrington, Michael & Leianne Flynn & Family, Sarah Forster, Michael J. Hedge, Liz Heinlein & Family, Renee & Brad Holmes, Jennifer Hurwitz, Heidi Jones, Sheila Kamuda, Michelle Kim, Carol Anne Kennedy, June Martin, David Miller, Carin Moore, Moose, Tom DesLongchamp, Steve & Janet Potter & Family, Joanna Price, Heidi & Jose Rodriguez, Diane Roger, Alie Satterlee, Sam T. Schick, Kirsten & Garrett Sessions, Andrea Summers, Brien Thompson, Helen Tsao, Anne Whiting, Kobi & Heidi Yamada & Family, Justi and Tote Yamada & Family, Bob and Val Yamada, Kaz & Kristin Yamada & Family, Tai & Joy Yamada, Anne Zadra, August & Arline Zadra, Dan Zadra, and Gus & Rosie Zadra.

CREDITS
Written & compiled by M.H. Clark
Designed by Jessica Phoenix

ISBN: 978-1-935414-11-7

1st Printing.   Printed in China with soy inks

These are the days of
miracle and wonder.

PAUL SIMON

Remember the feeling as a child when you woke up and morning smiled? It's time you felt like that again.

TAJ MAHAL

It is essential to our well-being, and to our lives, that we play and enjoy life. Every single day, do something that makes your heart sing.

MARCIA WIEDER

Each day provides its own gifts.

MARCUS AURELIUS

A multitude of small delights
constitutes happiness.

C H A R L E S   B A U D E L A I R E

Resolved, that I will take each
precious minute, and relish
all the joy within it.

KATHLEEN RICE

Tomorrow's life is too late. Live today.

Marcus Valerius Martialis

Joy is what happens to us when we allow ourselves to recognize how good things really are.

MARIANNE WILLIAMSON

◊ ◊ ◊

I thank you God for most this amazing day: for the leaping greenly spirits of trees and a blue true dream of sky; and for everything which is natural which is infinite which is yes.

E. E. CUMMINGS

If there's anything half
so much fun as being alive,
I'd like to know what it is.

MARY ENGELBREIT

When I asked for all things, so that I might enjoy life, I was given life, so that I might enjoy all things.

UNKNOWN

How simple it is to see that all the worry in the world cannot control the future. How simple it is to see that we can only be happy now. And that there will never be a time when it is not now.

GERALD JAMPOLSKY

We cannot cure the world of sorrows,
but we can choose to live in joy.

JOSEPH CAMPBELL

The gloom of the world is but a shadow;
behind it, yet within our reach, is joy.

FRA GIOVANNI GIOCONDO

Not knowing when the dawn will come, I open every door.

EMILY DICKINSON

The joy that you give to others
is the joy that comes back to you.

JOHN GREENLEAF WHITTIER

To be able to find joy in another's joy, that is the secret of happiness.

GEORGE BERNANOS

The more light you allow within
you, the brighter the world
you live in will be.

SHAKTI GAWAIN

There is no way to happiness.
Happiness is the way.

BUDDHA

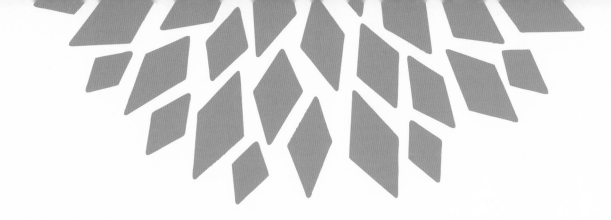

It is up to you to
illuminate the world.

PHILLIPPE VENIER

You have a gift that only you
can give the world—that's the
whole reason you're on the planet...
the miracle of your existence
calls for celebration every day.

OPRAH WINFREY

This very moment is a seed
from which the flowers of
tomorrow's happiness grow.

MARGARET LINDSEY

Paradise is where I am.

VOLTAIRE

Let a joy keep you. Reach out
your hands and take it
when it runs by.

CARL SANDBURG

When we understand that the secret of happiness lies not in possessing but in giving, by making others happy we shall be happier ourselves.

Andrew Gide

Those who wish to sing
always find a song.

SWEDISH PROVERB

Happiness often sneaks in through a door you didn't know you left open.

JOHN BARRYMORE

Let joy be unconfined.

LORD BYRON

Joy is not in things, it is in us.

RICHARD WAGNER ·

Some people are so much
sunshine to the square inch.

WALT WHITMAN